DON'T FORGET YOUR BONUSES!

Thanks for investing in a copy of *The Ultimate Property Listing*. I really appreciate it.

By way of thanks I'd like to give you a **FREE Ultimate Property Listing Checklist.**

Each item on the checklist is a helpful reminder of the methods I'll be outlining in this book. I use the checklist myself when creating listings for clients.

And that's not all! I'll also send you a **FREE Bonus Chapter** 'Taking Your Ultimate Property Listing Offline'.

This bonus chapter details how you can quickly and easily repurpose your Ultimate Property Listing to create real standout offline through direct mail.

DOWNLOAD YOUR FREE CHECKLIST & BONUS CHAPTER NOW!

www.ultimatepropertylisting.com/checklist

THE ULTIMATE PROPERTY LISTING: Create Powerful Estate & Letting Agency Listings To Grow Your Profits – Copyright © Neil Whitfield, 2021

All Rights Reserved. No part of this book may be reproduced in any form by any physical, electronic or mechanical means, including information storage and retrieval systems, without express permission in writing from the publisher, except by a reviewer who may quote brief passages in a review.

For more information please visit
www.ultimatepropertylisting.com

First Edition

First Edition: March 2021

This paperback edition first published in 2021

ISBN 9798577952198

CONTENTS

Who This Book Is For...**5**
What This Book Is Not..**7**
Introduction...**9**

Creating The Ultimate Property Listing

Ch. 1 – General Advertising Principles....................**12**
Ch. 2 – Property Advertising Basics.......................**15**
Ch. 3 – Price..**18**
Ch. 4 – Price As A Marketing Weapon...................**25**
Ch. 5 – Taking Photos (At The Property)...............**35**
Ch.6 – Photo Editing (Back At The Office)............**48**
Ch. 7 – Does Property Listing Copy Matter?.........**58**
Ch. 8 – Headlines That Get Attention....................**64**
Ch. 9 – The Full Description..................................**73**
Ch. 10 – Copy Length...**80**
Ch. 11 – Prove It!..**84**
Ch. 12 – Call To Action...**89**
Ch. 13 – Is It All Worth It?.....................................**91**
Ch. 14 – 3 Ultimate Property Listing Examples....**99**

Now What?

Ch. 15 – Property Power Words.............................**109**

Ch. 16 – The Next Step...**111**

About Neil Whitfield...**113**

A Small Favour..**116**

WHO THIS BOOK IS FOR

We both know that time is our most precious commodity. That's why I don't want to waste your valuable time if *The Ultimate Property Listing* is not for you.

I want to be 100% upfront and crystal clear about exactly who I wrote *The Ultimate Property Listing* for.

I wrote this book for **Open Minded** Estate Agents & Letting Agents. Agents who want to get better results from their listings – leading to more sales and more lets.

It's also worth adding that this book is for **Good** Estate & Letting Agents. Those who take pride in what they do. The agents who are always looking for ways to make improvements in the service they provide.

This book will challenge you and open your eyes to new ways of thinking about your listings and your wider agency business. So if you don't like to rock the boat or stick your head above the parapet, this book isn't for you.

I'm pretty plain speaking and call a spade a spade. So I'll say right now that I also wrote the book so that readers who '*get*' what I'm talking about can reach out to me if they think working together makes sense.

You OK with that? Good, let's crack on...

The *Ultimate Property Listing* Is For Agents Who:

- Have no interest in blindly conforming to traditional ways of working
- Are looking for a 'Slight Edge' to rise above their local competition
- Want to make the most out of what they've already got
- Are open minded and not afraid to try something new
- Understand small changes can deliver BIG results
- Can make decisions and implement them quickly
- Are ambitious and want to grow their business
- Are willing to invest in their business

Does that sound like you?

WHAT THIS BOOK IS NOT

This book is not a technical manual or 'Idiots Guide To Property Listings'. It doesn't show you how to upload a property picture onto to Rightmove, Zoopla or On The Market.

It would soon be out of date pretty quickly if it was.

It would only apply to the UK market.

It would also be a very dull book.

If you want that sort of basic advice, each portal or platform will have it's own User Guide and set of FAQs. Your web designer or administrator can help you if you're trying to fathom out the back end of your own website...

This book takes decades of advertising knowledge and applies it to your property listings.

It's a blend of specific tips on **What** to do and **How** to do it, combined with the strategic thinking behind it (so you understand the '**Why**').

That's why I hope this book will stand the test of time and transcend international borders.

It's worth establishing the limitations of this book. It's sole aim is to improve your property listings and increase the number of viewing requests from potential Buyers & Tenants.

It doesn't concern itself with how you follow up the enquiries. It offers no advice on what happens during the viewing. It doesn't help you with Sales progression. Or how you protect the tenancy deposit.

That said, improving your listings *will* improve your reputation. It *will* create a real point of difference in your crowded and competitive local market. So indirectly, it *will* benefit your business far beyond getting more clicks from your listings.

INTRODUCTION

Ever since the 19th century, advertisers have known what makes a good advert.

I'm not talking about the costly and un-trackable brand building ads. You know, the Big Brand 'Getting Our Name Out There' ads in the middle of Coronation Street.

A good ad should always seek to change behaviour.

Strangely, the tried and tested principles that have worked in every industry worldwide for over 100 years have never taken hold in UK property market.

Whether you're in Durham or Dartmouth, scan your local newspaper and you'll see identical ads from Estate Agents and Letting Agents.

They'll all have a list of bullet points. Showing "The Things That They Do" - which, let's face it, is 99% the same as everyone else in their town.

They'll list how long they've been going. They'll boast about their local knowledge.

They'll reference their "Passion", how much they "Care" and for them it's "Personal".

They'll tell you it's great that they've got an office in town. Or they'll tell you it's great they've **NOT** got an office in town.

This creates zero emotional connection with the reader. So it has little chance of getting them to change how they behave.

Why does it creates zero emotional connection with the reader?

Because it's all about the agent.

Face Facts. Very few people give two hoots about their Estate Agent or Letting Agent.

They care about themselves.

I know this because I enjoyed a successful 10 year career in direct response marketing. That's the branch of marketing that is 100% focused on changing behaviour and getting people to act in a certain way.

I worked for a couple of big International agencies. I helped create successful, award winning campaigns for brands like Rolls Royce, Energizer, McCain Foods, Nissan and RBS. I learned and applied the best battle-tested direct marketing principles. They worked.

In 2007 I quit marketing and bounded into the world of Lettings as the proud owner of a start-up agency.

It shocked me to see that all those years of advertising research and testing were being completely ignored.

And no more so that when it came to property listings...

Let's face it, whether it's your own home or a Buy To Let investment, a property is a pretty big asset. The highest value single item that most people are ever going to buy or sell.

If that's the case should property not be promoted in the best possible way? Using the very best advertising techniques available? To give the very best chance of success?

It would appear not.

This book will address this issue. It will show you how to create the Ultimate Property Listing and get people lining up to view your properties.

CHAPTER 1 – GENERAL ADVERTISING PRINCIPLES

The principles behind successful property advertising are no different to any other industry.

The role of advertising is to communicate ***what you have*** to those ***who may be interested*** in it. And to do so in a way that will ***persuade some of them to take action***.

In property you have a product (a house or flat) and you have potential customers (Buyers or Tenants). So far, so simple. In fact, the next two advertising principles are equally straightforward – but are also incredibly powerful.

A.I.D.A.

AIDA is an acronym that stands for **A**ttention, **I**nterest, **D**esire and **A**ction.

It describes the steps from a consumer first becoming aware of a product or service through to them making a buying decision.

AIDA dates back to the end of the 19th century and is so powerful and timeless that it's still widely used today.

It's used to develop complex marketing campaigns down to individual adverts, direct mail pieces or emails.

AIDA is a great framework to use when constructing an effective property listing. It works because each listing must take the reader through the four AIDA stages for them to arrange a viewing.

Attention – The property must stand out in the search results and get the attention of the reader.

Interest – The summary view info must get the reader to click through to the full listing.

Desire – The full listing must appeal to the heart and the head – to get the reader to consider the property.

Action – The reader must arrange a viewing.

It's frustrating and embarrassing how much advertising money is wasted because it doesn't follow this simple formula. In particular, so much 'money is left on the table' simply because advertisers rarely ask for Action.

Single Minded Objective

The sole aim of a property listing is to generate viewing requests.

Few agents understand that successful marketing activities must be single minded. **Always.**

They need to concentrate 100% on the One Thing they want to achieve. This means being laser focussed on how they are going to achieve it.

Instead, most agents mistakenly try to shove everything but the kitchen sink into one ad, leaflet or listing.

Chapter Summary

- Remember AIDA – first grab your reader's ATTENTION and get INTEREST
- They're most interested in THEMSELVES!
- Generate DESIRE by appealing to both their heart and head
- Finally ask for an ACTION – tell the reader what you want them to do
- Be single minded. Always

CHAPTER 2 – PROPERTY ADVERTISING BASICS

A successful property listing will generate viewing requests. And to request a viewing the potential buyer or tenant must go through two separate stages.

It's worth spelling out what needs to happen at each stage:

Search Results Summary - the summary information and photo that appear in the search results have one job to do. They must encourage potential Buyers or Tenants to click for more information.

I have deliberately written *potential* Buyers or Tenants above. There's no point in a family of four clicking through to see more information on a bedsit. Your summary information must attract those who are likely to be interested and repel those who are not.

Property Full Description – the property listing Full Description also has one job to do. It must encourage appropriate readers to request a viewing.

Click Through Rates

If your Search Result Summary gets 5,000 view per month with a Click Through Rate (CTR) of 5% you get 250 views of the full listing.

The more listing views you get, the more likely you are to get a viewing and the more likely you are to sell or let the property.

Increasing the Click Through Rate by a few percent can make a massive difference to your results.

If you take a poor performing property, getting 1% CTR and increase that to 5% then you'll go from 50 full listing views to 250.

Let's assume a conservative 5% of those looking at the listing will request a viewing. The above exercise will increase the number of viewings from 2.5 to 12.5.

Increasing a decent 5% CTR to 7% will deliver 350 listing views compared to 250 – resulting in five extra viewings.

Price, Photos & Search Results Copy

Rightmove research has identified the three factors that influence Click Through Rates. They are Price, Photos and the Search Result Summary Copy.

The data is based on Rightmove searches but it's generally accepted that the same principles will apply to the other portals, your website, Facebook Marketplace etc.

Aside from the stats, it just makes sense.

Over the next 11 chapters I'll break down the specific ways to optimise your listings.

You'll learn how to improve your Pricing Strategy, Photos and Copy to maximise Click Throughs. I'll then show you how to convert that interest into viewing requests.

Chapter Summary

- Always be on the lookout for ways to increase your Click Through Rate (CTR)
- Your Pricing Strategy, Photos and Search Results Copy have the most influence over your CTR

CHAPTER 3 – PRICE

Market Research & Local Knowledge

I assume you have experience in valuing properties For Sale & To Rent. I'm not going to teach you the basics of how to measure up, find the information on comparables, local area information and so on.

Instead, over the next two chapters you'll see that you have more scope to influence pricing than you currently think.

You are NOT entirely at the mercy of the market when determining the price to list a property.

Let's start with an easy one.

Furnished or Unfurnished?

Furnished rental properties are more expensive than Unfurnished, right? That was always the assumption.

Does this actually make sense? Does this still apply today?

Will a family with enough stuff to fill a 3-bed semi ever consider a furnished property?

Not unless it was so cheap that it the difference covered the cost of them putting an entire house full of stuff into storage...

Will a young couple with no furniture ever rent an unfurnished flat? Only if it was so cheap it would cover the cost of kitting out the whole flat with new furniture. On HP.

Even then it may be too much of a commitment. If a young couple are living together for the first time they can always go their separate ways at the end of the tenancy if it doesn't work out. But it's not as easy to get out of a four year Interest Free Credit agreement on a brand new sofa...

So the price of a Furnished property needs to reflect good value to those who don't have furniture. An Unfurnished property needs to reflect good value to those who do. It's not rocket science.

Then it comes down to the same things, location, condition, size, local amenities etc.

You need to look at all the above from the point of view of your Ideal Tenant.

An Unfurnished property near to a great school may be more attractive to a family than a Furnished property. So it can be priced at a premium.

But a young couple may pay more for a Furnished apartment in a trendy area with bars, restaurants and coffee shops. That's assuming the furnishings fit the aspirations of your ideal tenant. Not just any old tat.

Bills Included

When I started out, back in 2007, 'Bills Included' wasn't really "*A Thing*".

Now it's becoming increasingly popular and the range of Tenants asking for it is increasing.

A few years ago it was only students and HMO residents who would want a 'Bills Included' tenancy.

Now, those students are graduating and moving into 'normal' accommodation. Many like the lack of hassle that "Bills Included" living brings.

Because in my experience "Bills Included" is all about time and hassle. It's not about the money.

Yes, you do have the stereotypical students who sit around in their pants with the heating on full blast and all the windows open. But that's the exception rather than the norm.

Tenants want "Bills Included" because that's one less thing to worry about.

Who else could value having one less thing to worry about?

If you're renting to the cash strapped, it won't be for them. They're going to want to take complete control – to the extent of having prepayment meters rather than Bills Included.

But what about those who value time over money? The cash rich, time poor. Bills Included could be an interesting option to consider, whether that's for a luxury apartment or larger family home.

Because in offering this you're taking the property out of the 'No Bills' market.

You're making direct comparison with those 'No Bills' properties impossible. If the market is full of 'No Bills' properties then you may have found an angle to mark you out as somewhat different.

Bad Numbers

I laboured for some time about whether to include this section. I struggled because both points below struck me as 'Stating The Bleeding Obvious'. But a quick look on the portals proved that it is necessary. There's so many examples of "Bad Numbers" still being used.

It's possible to shoot yourself in the foot with pricing.

With Sales, pricing a property just over the Stamp Duty Land Tax (SDLT) threshold is a particularly short-sighted move. Your Buyers may think twice about offering, in case they're hit with a completely avoidable tax bill to pay.

You may struggle if your price is around this level as "Offers Over" or "Offers In The Region Of (OIRO)". Your potential Buyers may feel that they won't be able to negotiate the price down to under the SDLT level.

Depending on the strength of the market, anything up to £135,000 could scare off those wanting to avoid the 2% tax that starts at £125,001.

With all this in mind I've just seen a property on Rightmove which made me do a double take – why on earth would an agent price a property at £127,000?!?!?!?

Similarly with rentals, I've argued for many years that the way people search online means a rental price ending in 25 such as "£625pcm" shows the agent is a little bit thick...

I call this the Stupid £25 Pricing Strategy!

Most of the portals allow searchers to limit their searches based on £100 price bands. Most agents websites are similar...

The Stupid £25 Pricing Strategy is this;

Those searching 'Upto £600pcm' won't see a property priced at £625pcm.

If that's not bad enough, those with more to spend will be able to get something much bigger, better or in a nicer area for their money.

So the £625 property immediately becomes a poor relation compared to what else is affordable to them.

Price & Client Priorities

Most Vendors and Landlords will say that they want to achieve the highest price in the shortest time.

But you should press further. Because when you dig a little deeper, one of those – **Price** or **Speed** – will be much more important than the other.

Actually with rentals there's a further consideration. That's the quality of the Tenant.

Price has a part to play in all these. You normally have to trade off one (or two) to achieve the other.

It's your role to get under the skin of each Landlord or Vendor. You need to determine what the one most important factor is for them at this moment in time.

"*At this moment in time*" is crucial. You need to be aware that the importance they place may change over time.

Think of the stereotypical motivated seller. He's just had his second consecutive sale fall through and he's worried that he'll lose his dream home. Now he'll want a quick sale, even if it means taking a very low offer.

Nine months ago he would have told you that he was in no rush, as long as he got the highest price

He'll not thank you for holding out on price now – not when he needs a quick sale.

But don't ever assume that Vendors and Landlords will offer this up to you, should you fail to ask. Always assume that it will be 100% *Your Fault* if the deal falls through, or you lose out to another agent who was more attentive to their immediate needs.

Chapter Summary

- Price according to what is good value for the Ideal Tenant
- Price can open up a whole new market e.g. Bills Included
- Never shoot yourself in the foot with Bad Numbers
- Don't assume your Landlords or Vendors will tell you if their pricing priorities change. Ask them. Often

CHAPTER 4 – PRICE AS A MARKETING WEAPON

Anyone who's read a Marketing textbook will know Price is one of the traditional marketing 4P's. The others are Place, Promotion and Product.

The 4P's are a bit simple, outdated and irrelevant for most small businesses nowadays. That said, at least it highlights that Price has place in your marketing toolkit.

You might have studied for years to be a RICS qualified chartered surveyor. You may be providing letting valuations based on local comparables with a bit of gut feel thrown in. Either way, it's worth reiterating that the a property is only worth what someone will pay for it.

How many times have you heard Landlords or Vendors convinced that their property is 'worth' far more than the ceiling for the street or the area?

It happens because it's far too easy to get obsessed with Features and Benefits. Do that and you risk ignoring why your customers are actually looking to Buy or Rent.

That usually involves moving *towards pleasure* or *away from pain*. More on this later.

In this chapter I'll show you that price can make your listing stand out. I'll also suggest some promotional pricing ideas that may provide a real point of difference.

These ideas won't work for all properties. I'm also not suggesting you attempt them all at once! But where appropriate, they can be a useful way to achieve stand out and differentiation.

Promotional Pricing

Before opening my letting agency in 2007 I enjoyed 10 years developing marketing campaigns for a range of brands.

This gave me exposure to a wide range of promotional pricing techniques – most often used with Fast Moving Consumer Goods for clients like McCain Foods, Energizer, Wilkinson Sword, Aunt Bessie's and Rustlers (They're 0-Tasty in 70 seconds!!).

Launch Pricing

Launch pricing is often used to generate initial interest in many industries. It works in both Business to Business (B2B) and Business to Consumer (B2C).

You want to get most interest when first listing a property For Sale or To Rent. So it makes sense to incentivise the early birds to view, apply or make an offer to take advantage of a preferential, won't-be-around-forever price.

"It's £500pcm if you apply in the next 14 days then it goes up to £550pcm"

"£650pcm based on a move-in date before 31st January"

"£150,000 until 1st June then £155,000 after that"

Why hasn't this promotional pricing strategy taken hold in property?

Is it because price (even in Lettings) is still all very factual, scientific and linear? Determined by square footage, property features, local amenities etc?

In property it's not seen as a variable plaything of the Agent, Vendor or Landlord. It's not viewed as something to be tweaked and nudged to meet market demand.

But then if a property has been on the market for some time a price reduction is one of the most powerful ways to revive interest.

It's also understood that holding out for a month or two to get an extra £50 (Rentals) or £5,000 (Sales) often doesn't make sense. Not when you factor in the lost income, holding expenses, losing out on the ideal property etc.

We also know that FOMO (Fear Of Missing Out) is a very powerful weapon. Genuine scarcity is a great way to encourage action.

All this adds weight to my argument that you must make the very most of the *shiny newness* of a property when it is first listed. Don't wait months before using price as a way to influence demand.

Having a launch price is a great way to capitalise and cash in on that initial period of greatest interest.

Especially if the property has a lot of competition or really isn't all that special.

Link it to a strong call to action – ACT NOW OR PAY MORE!

Longer Let Pricing

Tenants are staying longer and looking for longer tenancies. Legislation may come in that forces Landlords & Agents to offer longer tenancies. So far, so straightforward.

So why don't advertised prices reflect this preference for longer term tenancies?

I'm sure you've all had conversations with Landlords, negotiating a lower rent for a longer term tenancy.

You should know if your Landlords are open to longer tenancies (assuming their mortgage allows them). Many will actually prefer a longer let.

If you know this then why do as everyone else does and advertise the property at the 6 month tenancy rate?

I know it's how things are normally advertised. But it doesn't make sense!

Why not promote a price based on a two year let, discounted to reflect the certainty and security this gives the Landlord?

If people don't want or can't commit to this longer term then they pay a little more for a six month let. The tables are turned and they negotiate a higher rent for a shorter tenancy!

If you lease a car for three years you pay a lot less per day than hiring it for a week...

The effect of this on the search results can be pretty significant. Don't forget the role of a property listing is simply to get the viewing...

Imagine a potential Tenant is comparing five similar properties next to each other on a portal. Four are at the market rent of £850pcm and one is at £795. They all look as attractive as each other. Which one will get the most interest and the most clicks?

If the cheaper property gets an application one month earlier on a two year let that brings in an extra £795 rent payment. That covers £795 of the £1,320 (24 months x £55) 'lost' in offering the lower rent.

That only leaves £525 to cover before renting at the lower amount generates a higher return in the long run.

Factor in the voids, potential relet fees saved, not to mention the wear and tear which comes from people moving in and out...

The strategy of taking a lower rent starts to look like making commercial sense for some Landlords.

The property listing needs to be upfront about the longer term tenancy pricing at the earliest opportunity.

This is to avoid any accusations of underhand tactics or misleading potential Tenants.

But given many people are looking for longer term lets, when the pricing model is understood it's going to be seen as a POSITIVE rather than a negative.

Odd Numbers

Why are Estate Agents and Letting Agents so po-faced and serious about pricing and valuations?

I've been in business for over 25 years and I've learned that it becomes a lot more enjoyable and also more profitable if you don't take it quite so seriously. I'm not suggesting being foolish or unprofessional. Far from it. But perhaps just lighten up a touch...

You see it's all a bit of a game. You set a price on behalf of your Landlord or Vendor. If you're any good, you should get plenty of interest, offers or applications.

But how many Sales actually go through with the Buyer paying exactly the advertised price? Most of the time people will haggle for a reduction or even offer higher to secure a sought after property...

So if it hardly ever sells for the advertised amount why get so hung up about the price?

A lot of the time it's because agents use the price of the property as a way to win the business.

But to paraphrase Seth Godin *"If your customers only care about price, you haven't given them anything more interesting to care about"*.

Develop strong, compelling reasons for Landlords & Vendors to choose you. That way you won't ever have to use the price to win the business.

Instead why not use the property price as a Pattern Interrupt? That's something that makes the searcher stop and pay attention. Catch them for that split second and you might then tempt them to read the headline and click for more info.

The role of a listing is to get a viewing. The role of the Search Result Summary info, including the price, is to get the click.

So when I say 'Odd Numbers' I really mean peculiar, unexpected numbers. The kind that catches the eye because it looks odd, not because it ends in a three, five or seven.

If you're faced with being one of 25 similar properties all advertised at £125,000 why not put it on at £124,567.89

Because your Estate Agency mates at the Golf Club would laugh at you?

Really? Who cares?

Why are 99% of rentals advertised at prices ending in 00, 25, 50, 75 and 95?

Stick a 97 in there, a 34 or an 89.99

Many astute readers will be noticing a couple of trends in the advice I'm giving throughout this book.

I'm not a one for blindly following convention. And I'm not afraid of looking silly. Because I know this works.

"First they ignore you, then they laugh at you, then they fight you, then you win." Mahatma Ghandi

There are plenty of quick and easy ways to make your listing standout. Often it does require stepping out of your comfort zone. It means sticking your head above the parapet. Trying something a bit *Out There*.

If you sell or let their property in record time, or for more than they expected – will your Landlords or Vendors care that your methods were a little bit odd?

Cashback

This one's for lettings. I must start by saying I'm generally not a fan of Joint Agency at all. It encourages the completely wrong attitude towards Tenant selection. First with a pulse...

Anyway, if you absolutely must do Joint Agency, for God's sake don't fight fair! You used to be able to slash your fee to make your agency most attractive. Now you can't do that.

You can alter the price in another way – give Cashback. It doesn't need to be much - £50 will do it. But on a

Fully Managed property the £50 'lost' is far outweighed by the potential of management fees for years to come.

Chapter Summary

- Longer Let pricing can make your property stand out as a bargain AND appeal to both Landlords & Tenants
- If you really must do Joint Agency, stack the cards in your favour with Cashback on Managed lets
- Launch pricing can capitalise on and convert initial interest
- Don't blindly follow the crowd. Try some *Odd Numbers*

CHAPTER 5 – TAKING PHOTOS (AT THE PROPERTY)

I must start this chapter by stating loud and clear **I AM NOT A PROFESSIONAL PHOTOGRAPHER**.

This chapter is a mix of advice and experience I've accumulated over the years. Learning from property photography experts plus my 10+ years listing properties as a Letting Agent.

Wherever the advice is specific or technical, it's safe to assume I've lifted it from a professional!

I've broken the photography section down into two chapters. This one covers what you need to do at the property. The following chapter covers what you need to do back at the office.

Camera Equipment

The first question to address when discussing photography equipment is "Camera vs. Phone?"

I've seen great property photos taken on a phone and I've seen terrible photos taken on a very expensive camera.

That said, if you want to maximise the interest generated by your listings you need to invest in a camera. Never take your marketing photos on a phone.

During the 10 years I owned my letting agency I tended to favour a Panasonic Lumix compact camera.

It was relatively cheap (under £300), small and had a built in wide angle lens. Having the built in wide angle lens meant we didn't need to faff about with lugging extra lenses around.

This camera could fit in your jacket pocket. But it still allowed our photos to be much better than 99.9% of our local competitors.

That said, things have moved on – so my advice now is to get a DSLR (Digital Single Lens Reflex) camera with a specific wide angle lens.

Entry level DSLR cameras from Canon & Nikon start around £200 - £300 for the camera (no lens). The more whizzy, feature-packed Intermediate cameras are closer to £1,000.

Either way, you'd then have to budget a further £300 - £350 for the wide angle lens.

A wide angle lens is an absolute MUST for property photography. You'll need one to create a wide enough shot of a room to make it attractive and show the space in a room.

That said there's nothing worse than 'All The Gear, No Idea' so if you've splashed out over £500 on kit you may want to invest a little more in training to get the most out of it.

You DO NOT ever want a fish-eye lens! It's like looking at an image on the back of a spoon. Try it with your own face and a spoon!

Tripods

The next question with equipment is "To Tripod or not to Tripod?".

I managed to get great results without a tripod. But there are those who insist a tripod is an absolute necessity.

It may sound obvious but a tripod is there to make sure the image is not blurred. If you can find a way to deliver this without a tripod then you'll be much quicker without it.

If you're Mr Shaky Hands (an obscure 1990's TV 'Banzai' reference...) then invest in a tripod.

If not, here's how to get the camera still and steady without a tripod.

Crouch down and wedge yourself into a corner. Lean back against the walls. Raise the camera to your face and keep it level. Now you're crouching the camera should be around waist height if you were in a standing position.

Crouching in the corner should lead you to aiming the camera across the room to the other corner.

Now lock your elbows against the 'V' of the walls or whatever surface is handy. You'll give yourself a solid frame from which to take the photo. If you can't do that I used to hold my non-clicking hand under the camera for extra support.

Finally, when you're about to take the photo, hold your breath. Seriously. I've seen this bit of advice mocked on various forums but it makes perfect sense. Breathing will affect your body, so it may create a small movement that can have an impact on the photo.

If it's good enough for an Olympic gold medal winning marksman, it's good enough for an Estate Agent in Slough...

I want to labour the point that you should always be taking shots at around waist height. Even in small rooms like bathrooms or the downstairs loo. Never feel tempted to do that Hold-It-Up-A-Height-And-Point-Downwards thing.

I conducted an unscientific poll in a Facebook letting agent group recently. Asking the simple question "Tripod or Crouch?". The results were interesting.

Pretty much an even split but slightly in favour of tripods. There was a definite bias towards tripods from the middle aged men – citing dodgy knees as the main factor!

If you do decide to buy a tripod don't go for the cheapest option you can get from China on the internet.

Chances are it will be flimsy and unstable or it will break. And you don't want to risk damaging your expensive camera and lens because of a cheap tripod failure. Go for a decent reputable brand.

For internal shots set the tripod so the camera is around 1.2m off the ground. You'll need to increase this to 1.5m to get above the work surfaces in the kitchen. For external shots you should aim to be even higher, up to 1.8m.

Lighting

I've seen Sales agents lugging around masses of lighting equipment. I'd suggest all professional photographers will use some form of lighting equipment.

But I never used any artificial lighting.

It sounds obvious but one of the key things is to make sure you're taking photos when the natural light is good. Not too bright but not too dim. It's far easier to sort out a photo that's too dark but it's much harder to do so if the original is too light.

If you do need to turn the lights on in the property do so and wait. Let them warm up to full brightness.

I would always take a series of photos with the lights on and also with the lights off. You can never tell on-site what is going to be best and it gives you options when you're back at the office.

When taking external photos never shoot with the sun shining straight into the lens. Too much light can be very difficult to fix. You may need to come back at a different time to get the best possible external photos. You can even download an app which will tell you the ideal time to photograph your property!

The Basics

I'm often appalled by the "Crimes Against Photography" committed by agents who should know better!

There's a notable multi-branch agent close to me who have a habit of taking exterior photos from inside the car. With the window up.

If the weather is so bad you can't get out of the car then should you be taking photos in the first place?

Are you so busy that you don't even have time to step out of the car?

There's no excuse for this.

It's hardly presenting the property in the best light to attract Buyers or Tenants. And will any prospective Landlord or Vendor who sees this listing think 'They're the agent for me!'

It comes down to planning. Make sure you allow enough time to take good quality photos inside and outside the property.

It will take more time to photograph a five bedroom detached with extensive grounds than a one bed studio.

But even with a small studio or flat it should take you at least 20 minutes. For larger properties it could take an hour or more to get it right.

Preparation

It may be my own personal OCD coming to light but I would never publish a shot of a bathroom where the toilet seat was up. Or an outside front shot on bin day. I've sent staff members back to properties to correct such small things (Boss Of The Year 2013...).

Preparation is vital. It's also something most of your competitors won't bother with. So by getting this right you will stand out. Yes, even with Rentals...

Get permission to temporarily remove items so the shot looks as good as possible. Then 100% make sure you put everything back where you found it.

Remove all bathroom shampoos, shower gels, toothpaste, bleach, cleaning products, towels, lotions and potions.

In the kitchen, leave the work surfaces as clean and clear as possible.

Remove everything but the toaster, microwave and kettle. Remove the oven gloves and tea towels from the radiator or the oven door.

Clear away little Archie's charming artwork stuck to the fridge. Also hide the washing up liquid, scourers or cloths.

Remove everything but an attractive fruit bowl or vase from the kitchen or dining room table.

With living rooms and bedrooms it's often harder to remove the occupier's personal effects. But keep things that shouldn't be there to a minimum or hidden.

Ironing boards, piles of laundry, exercise equipment, that sort of thing. And make the bed!

With experience, you'll get to know what's going to be visible in the final shot and what isn't.

This often means you don't have to remove things completely, you can often get away with scooting them behind a bed or piece of furniture...

One final piece of advice on preparation. From the outset be strict with your Landlords & Vendors about what you expect from them.

Give them a checklist of what they need to do before the photo-shoot. Tidying up, removing items, painting etc. Stick to your guns if they haven't lived up to their end of the bargain.

Call them the day before to check they've done everything. If they haven't, rearrange the photo-shoot.

If you're in any doubt, ask them to take a quick couple of photos on their phone and send them over to you. Your time is precious so be firm.

Dressing & Staging

I never used a staging company to dress a property before taking photos or doing viewings. Now there are very cost effective ways to do this digitally (more on this later).

We had a duvet set with pillows and cushions in a big blue IKEA bag. We would take it to furnished properties where they looked a bit stark and basic.

It's amazing the difference a duvet cover and matching pillows makes compared to a plain mattress on a bed. A couple of cushions on a sofa and a vase on a table can make a room look much more homely and welcoming.

Test Shots

I was never taught this but to me it makes sense. Before taking the 'real' shots in each room I would always get myself into position and take a test shot.

I'd then study the shot on the screen of my camera. That way I could spot visible items, check the lighting was OK, think about moving furniture etc.

Having the discipline to do this in every room added around 5-10 minutes to each photo session. But it saved much more time by reducing the amount of editing needed back at the office. I've no doubt that it was a major factor in our producing excellent property photos.

Composition

If you're crouching in a corner then that will lead you to shoot towards the opposite corner of the room.

With small rooms or where you can't wedge yourself into a corner I've would stand outside the room. I'd shoot into the room through the open door towards the opposite corner. I developed a handy skill of using my front kneeling foot to wedge open the door so it didn't appear in shot.

Property photography is often best done alone because some of the positions you have to contort your body into are not always best shared with an audience...

I've heard some photographers say you should never have a window in the shot. Others say never show an internal door. Do what works for you.

It's up to you whether to have a window in the shot or not. But you should always avoid auto-focusing on the window. Given this is the lightest part of the room, if you do focus on it the rest of the room will look very dark.

When taking external shots they always tend to look better taken from an angle rather than face on. Especially if there's a front garden or drive. I'd even take this approach with mid-terrace properties.

How Many Photos?

I recall training an experienced Negotiator on 'My Way' of taking photos.

It surprised me that she would only take one shot of each room 'to save time'. More often than not she would check the photo on the screen of the camera to make sure it wasn't blurred.

But not always.

There were still occasions where she would have to return to the property. Because she'd only notice once she got back to the office, this turned into a very costly and time consuming exercise.

I impressed upon her that this 'time saving' exercise was wasting her valuable time.

I joked that with digital photography it didn't cost any more to take 100 shots than it did one.

I was mindful that when she started out in property it would have been necessary to get a film developed, print out physical photos and glue them to an A4 sheet to stick in the window (at this point anyone under 30 is probably scratching their heads...).

So as a guide I would always take 3-5 'Good' shots of each angle, of each room. This is having already undertaken the test shot exercise outlined earlier.

Outside try different angles and different distances. Alter the main focal point in the foreground.

For the rear garden I would also shoot away from and facing the property, straight-on and from many angles.

You're aiming to have at least 5 – 9 superb photos per property.

Chapter Summary

- Lighting is important. Too dark can be fixed much easier than too light
- For best results use a DSLR camera and Tripod
- Take multiple shots per room
- Always take a test shot
- Prepare the room

CHAPTER 6 – PHOTO EDITING (BACK AT THE OFFICE)

The principles from Chapter 5 will make your photos much better than your competition.

But you'd be missing a trick if you clicked 'Upload' and started using them without first improving them.

Photo Editing Software

I'm assuming most agents don't use professional paid-for editing software like Adobe Photoshop.

My recommendations work on both PC and Mac with FREE software.

For many years I used Google's free photo editing software **Picasa**. It's a great bit of software that balances being easy-to-use but powerful. They stopped supporting it in the last couple of years but you can still get hold of Picasa3 from selected download sites.

If you don't want to use Picasa3 then **paint.net** or **pixlr.com** are good, free alternatives. They all work on both PC or Mac. For those who want to process their images on the go, **Adobe Lightroom** is free to use on mobile devices.

Simple Photo Editing

You need to perform a few simple operations to make your photos crisp, clear and make the colours jump off the page. All the above packages will allow you to do this.

I won't get into how to remove competitors boards, make your grass green or turn a grey sky into blue with fluffy white clouds. That's far too technical for me. You can either learn these skills on YouTube or send your images away to have them improved (more on this later).

Instead, I'm going to cover the basics that will still make a big difference to how your images appear on-screen.

The first thing you need to do is sharpen the image. Even if you've followed all the instructions from the last chapter, there's a big difference between 'not blurry' and 'sharp'.

Next you should look at the lighting of the shot. You can lighten a photo that's too dark without too much trouble but it's much harder to deal with too much light. When you're doing this operation always be careful not to 'bleach' the shot with too much light.

You should also look at the colour of the shot, the warmth and the highlights. Getting the balance right is crucial to making your images jump off the screen.

You don't want to make a white room look like it's been lived in by a 40-a-day smoker! So when dealing with white rooms be extra careful when altering the colour and warmth.

The search result thumbnail image will be very small (especially if viewed on a tablet or mobile phone). That's why I would always alter the colour, warmth and highlights so they were vivid and vibrant. Hyper-real.

That said, you need to find a balance. It needs to 'pop' on-screen without looking too much like a 1990's Altern8 video.

I remember a local competitor who always got it very wrong in this way.

It was very hard to put a finger on why his efforts didn't work and ours did. He was trying to replicate our 'house style' and had all the tools at his disposal but he just didn't have the eye for it.

Without knowing what package you're using it's hard to be specific on what buttons to press and what sliders to slide.

The adjustments you should be making will be covered by the following terms. Have a play and get to know what looks good and what jumps off the page when scaled down to the size of a summary view thumbnail.

- Sharpness
- Lightness
- Brightness
- Contrast
- Temperature
- Tint
- Hue
- Saturation
- Highlights
- Shadows

Once you get the hang of it you should be able to do all this in a couple of minutes per photo.

Professional Photo Editing

If you want to get more advanced then you'll need to send your images out to a professional. It doesn't make sense to spend hours slaving over them when you can outsource for less than £1 an image and get them back within 24h.

There are many companies who provide retouching services. They'll also provide virtual furnishing, 3D tours and floor plans.

Just a note on virtual furnishing – earlier I mentioned staging rooms prior to photos being taken. Now technology allows you to digitally 'dress' a room with a huge range of furniture and complementary accessories.

This won't be appropriate or necessary for all properties but if you've got an unoccupied property that's looking stark, or want to offer an Unfurnished property as Furnished, this may be a very cost effective solution.

For all of the above I highly recommend Doctor Photo **www.dctr.co.uk** the UK's longest established property photo processing specialists. I'm not on any commission for this, I just get along well with them and they're good at what they do.

Photo Order

The order you show your photos on the property listing does make a big difference.

You'll get to show 1-3 photos before the viewer has to click to see the rest.

Before getting into detail I want to cover off one thing that I see so many agents getting wrong. Something so simple yet so powerful.

If you just apply one learning from this book to make a big difference to your listings then let it be this one…

Tenants really don't care about what the front of the house looks like.

I spot this time and time again. It must be a throwback to Sales agents always leading with the exterior front shot. And that's fine for them to do so – because Buyers do tend to be more concerned about the 'Curb Appeal' of a property.

But for Lettings – if you show the front of the property you are shooting yourself in the foot. You'll always get a higher click through rate if you use an internal shot as the Lead Photo.

It's bad practice to lead with the exterior shot for rental houses but even worse if it's an apartment in a block.

So you go with the best room as the lead shot. More often than not that will be the living room or the kitchen.

After that think about what's going to be most appealing and attractive to entice that click. So if you've led with either the living room or kitchen, the second shot should be the other one.

Then the main bedroom. Then the bathroom. Notice that I've still haven't said the exterior front yet...

If you have a rear garden then that comes next. The logic being to break up the roll of internal photos with a bit of greenery. Otherwise you'll have a lot of mainly magnolia, grey or white images. It's also worth putting the back garden in here to get them thinking about how they may use and enjoy that outside space...

Then go throughout the property room by room and leave the exterior front shot to last. The major portals suggest you have at least seven shots to maximise appeal.

Think that's going to be impossible with a one bedroom apartment? Why not use shots taken from different angles in the most attractive rooms? Or the hall. Or even the communal areas, if they are attractive.

Captivating Captions

If a photo speaks a thousand words, what about a photo *that also contains a few words*?

Advertisers have known for decades that adding a caption to a photo will increase the engagement. In recent years adding captions to photos has taken hold on social media posts and stories. So why do so few agents use this technique on their listing photos?

Adding captions is easy using free software like **www.canva.com** and can really make your lead photo jump out in the search results summary.

When adding a caption keep it short. Three or four words at most. The caption should really mirror the key benefit being described in the Short Description copy.

A word of caution. You're at the mercy of the portal platforms allowing this. At the time of writing it seems to be OK but this may change. If it does, then there's nothing to stop you from continuing to use captions on your own website and social media.

Special Effects

If you're looking to make a property photo stop someone in their tracks, make it a *drawing*.

There's plenty of free tools and apps where you can upload a photo then apply all manner of creative effects that will make it jump off the screen.

I use the Art Filter app on Android but there are loads to choose from.

You can turn your photo into:

- A black and white photo
- A watercolour painting
- An abstract painting
- A pencil sketch

There are literally hundreds of effects available.

I tried this on a selection of properties a few years back. It had a positive impact on the click through rates, increasing most by a couple of percentage points.

But it seemed to tail off after a few weeks. Perhaps the novelty factor wore off...?

That said, there's a constant flow of new Buyers and Tenants coming into the market so it may be something to consider on selected properties every few months.

Chapter Summary

- Image sharpness and vibrant colours are most important to create standout
- Consider outsourcing for more complex editing and retouching
- Consider captions and special effects for increased standout
- Never lead with the outside front for Lettings
- Always edit your shots prior to uploading
- Photo order is very important

CHAPTER 7 – DOES PROPERTY LISTING COPY MATTER?

Copy is one of the most controversial property listing topics.

Many agents refuse to accept that property listing copy is worth worrying about. One agent even recalled a long period where his listings didn't have ANY property descriptions.

"It made no difference", he said.

I come from a direct marketing background. In this world copy is king.

The best copywriters can command 6 figures for writing a single sales letter or landing page!

I firmly believe well written property listing copy can make a BIG difference.

And for those agents who think photos are the most important part of a property ad? Legendary adman HW Hepner put it far better than I could;

"Catching attention should lead to capturing the mind. Effective advertising means that the reader's mind as well as his eye must be captured."

And to capture the mind, you need good copy.

Zillow Talk

Still unconvinced? Let me share some revealing statistical research from the US real estate behemoth, Zillow.

Zillow is the worlds largest real estate site. It gets over 90 million visits per month and has data on over 110 million US homes.

They looked at 24,000 home sales. They measured how different words, descriptions and even the listing length affected the sale price.

They noted that certain words corresponded to higher prices being achieved. Words such as 'Captivating' tended to beat their expected sale price by 6.5%. 'Granite' was linked to higher than expected sale prices in both bottom, middle and top tier homes (the difference ranging from 1.1% to 4.2%).

Other words such as 'Investment', 'Potential' and 'Bargain' led to lower than expected prices being achieved.

Based on this research, the words you use can be worth thousands of pounds.

Unfortunately few UK based agents know how to write good listing copy that can make a difference. And they don't see the benefit because all their competitors are doing it the same way too. There's nothing to compare against.

I'm saying 'You Don't Know What You Don't Know' more and more these days. It applies here. If you don't know there is another (better) way then how can you seek it out?

I'm also drawn to this quote from Henry Ford, who knew a thing or two about mass transportation *"If I had asked people what they wanted, they would have said faster horses"*.

People tend to favour small improvements in what they know, accept and understand. They don't look 'outside the box' for new, groundbreaking ways of doing things.

But it goes even deeper than that.

Many agents are getting confirmation bias about copy from their Buyers and Tenants.

Their Buyers or Tenants will say that the copy is the same, full of jargon and that they don't pay it much attention.

That's because it DOES all look and sound the same! Because it IS all full of jargon!

Buyers and Tenants get used to wading through bland, cliché and jargon ridden copy. It doesn't tell them much and doesn't connect with them. So they learn to switch off or skim over the copy.

This presents you with a great opportunity to stand out.

The bar will be so low that even a small improvement will lift your listing way above your competitors.

"In The Kingdom Of The Blind, The One Eyed Man Is King…" Desiderius Erasmus

But there are other benefits, besides engaging with your potential Buyers or Tenants. Crafting your listing copy can help you to attract Landlords & Vendors.

One of my soapbox issues that I'll rant about for hours is agents having little or no real point of difference. This means Landlords and Vendors struggle to tell one agent from another. So they base their decisions on price.

I call it "**Vanilla Sludge**".

The frustrating thing is, there are plenty of ways to differentiate your agency. Such as becoming known locally for your well written, interesting listings.

OK…that alone may not win you an instruction – but it gets more interesting if you Productise this process.

What do I mean by *Productise*?

Instead of saying 'We'll take some photos, write a description then put them all online' what if you could offer:

Your unique, "15 point Tenant Attraction Process (TAP)"

Will your annoying competitor be able to offer to "Turn On The TAP" in this way? Nope.

Will it give you something special and memorable? Something that renders like-for-like price comparison much more tricky? Sure will.

Look, I know that a lot of what you're doing to market a property will be the same as your competitors.

But break it down into named stages with a couple of real points of difference thrown in. Do that and you can start to lift your agency out of the Vanilla Sludge.

Chinese Whispers

Who writes your listing copy?

Ultimately who writes the copy is not important. What is important is that they have been to the property.

They also must understand who the target Buyer or Tenant is and specifically what they are looking for.

Often the job of writing the listing is delegated to someone who hasn't been to the property at the time of writing the listing.

They're therefore limited to regurgitating cold, hard facts. This leads to dull listings that don't connect emotionally.

Don't fall into this trap.

I really don't care whether the MD, Lister, Valuer or Junior Admin person writes the listing copy. As long as they've been to the property and understand the needs of their target audience.

Chapter Summary

- Property listing copy is very important
- Well written copy can differentiate your Agency and transmits a Quality approach that will get noticed
- The person writing the copy must have been to the property AND understand the needs of the target Buyer or Tenant

CHAPTER 8 – HEADLINES THAT GET ATTENTION

The Short Description is the two or three lines of copy that comes up in the search results summary.

Recalling AIDA from earlier – it is incredibly important.

That's because it will affect the number of clicks that your property receives. And so it directly affects the number of viewings requested.

But more often than not, half the valuable Short Description character count is wasted.

"Blah De Blah Estates are proud to receive instruction and bring to the market this well presented..."

That's 97 characters wasted.

97 characters that tell me nothing about the property. 97 characters that say nothing about why the property may interest **ME**.

You might only get 250 characters for the 'Short Description' on some UK portals.

I've just seen this complete waste of the entire Short Description on Zoopla:

"Well presented and very much a welcomed addition to the market for sale. With high levels of interest anticipated, we would strongly recommend internal inspection to fully appreciate. Offering spacious living accommodation throughout this pleasant..."

The above is a truly shocking example. Even so it's rare to see the Short Description copy saying anything that looks anything like a 'proper' ad headline. And that's a real missed opportunity.

Let me explain.

Headlines are super important.

All the expert studies agree on one thing – the headline can make or break an ad. It's the headline that draws you in and determines whether you stop to read more.

The Short Description copy is the Headline for a property listing.

You can have the most well written property description but that won't help if your ideal Tenant scrolls right by...

If the lead photo doesn't immediately capture interest or attention you have one more opportunity to stop the viewer in their tracks before they scroll on. The Short Description.

The Short Description needs to Get Attention.

Most of the portals will pull through what the property is i.e. '3 bedroom semi-detached', '2 bedroom apartment' and where it is – either the area or the street.

With that in mind, why repeat all this in the Short Description? It's a further waste of valuable characters.

So, by taking out the 'Proud to be instructed' name check, the property type and where it is you can list all the main property features in the Short Description headline, right?

Wrong.

That's Me!

You want your ideal Buyer or Tenant to stop scrolling and one of the best ways to do that is if they think 'That's Me!'

An easy way to get attention is to call out your ideal Buyer or Tenant at the start of the Short Description.

Young Couples!

Families With Kids!

Downsizers!

Party Animals!

That would be 100% more powerful than the start of most Short Descriptions.

But it's getting dangerously close to that cliché classic attention-grabber so beloved by Letting Agents

Attention Landlords!

If you give it a little more thought you can do so much better than that.

Moving Towards Pleasure

The reader needs to visualise the positive transformation that the property will have on their life.

People generally make decisions based on emotion then justify with fact and logic. And yet 99% of all property ads contain nothing but the facts!

Think about how the property will increase or improve one of the following for the Buyer or Tenant?

- **Mental** – Does the property have calming sea views? Is it close to the countryside or a pleasant park?
- **Physical** – Does the property have an open plan kitchen and living area? Is it ideal for entertaining? What must-have gym facilities are in the building

- **Financial** – Is this a cracking little investment? Does it have an efficient solar powered heating system that will save the buyer a fortune in bills?
- **Social** – Will their friends be jealous? Is this one of the most sought-after places to live?
- **Emotional or Spiritual** – Will moving here reduce stress by halving their commute
- **Security** – How will this property protect them and their loved ones? Does it have a big fence? Is it likely to go up in value?

Moving Away From Pain

Moving towards pleasure is a powerful motivator. Tapping into the above examples should make for effective Short Descriptions.

But a transformation that moves ***away from pain*** is even more likely to motivate and change behaviour.

How will the property allow the Buyer or Tenant to avoid (reduce or eliminate) the following

- Risks
- Worries
- Losses
- Mistakes

- Embarrassment
- Drudgery or some other undesirable condition

Often you can look at the positives and flip them to create a negative. But be careful with negatives. You don't want to leave them feeling too bad!

A powerful technique is to ask a question that forces the reader to picture themselves in the situation.

It's powerful because the reader will struggle NOT to think about it, answer it or visualise it.

Don't think about a purple elephant.

We can look again at the Young Couples and Families With Kids... call-out examples used earlier.

See how much more powerful a relevant question or involving statement could be. This works whether it's gaining a positive or removing a negative:

Imagine Your 3 Minute Weekend Stroll Down To Your Favourite Cafe

Your Friends Will Be SO Jealous When They Hear Where You've Moved!

Sick & Tired Of Creeping In Late So You Don't Wake Your Parents?

Is Your Tiny Flat Bursting At The Seams?

The longest of those is 67 characters...

Having got their attention you now need to give them a compelling reason to click through. You do that by relating the most appropriate property features to the question posed. Like this:

Imagine Your 3 Minute Weekend Stroll Down To Your Favourite Cafe. Ideally located a short walk from the leafy and fashionable...

Your Friends Will Be SO Jealous When They Hear Where You've Moved! This stunning apartment in the exclusive and sought after _____ development...

Sick & Tired Of Creeping In Late So You Don't Wake Your Parents? Gain your independence with this affordable 1 bedroom flat...

Is Your Tiny Flat Bursting At The Seams? This spacious semi is ideal for growing families...

Title Case

Did you notice that in the examples above the first letter of each word in the first sentence was a capital?

That's called Title Case. It's been found to increase readability and engagement.

It's widely used offline in direct marketing and online in both Google and Facebook ads. It's far better than the spammy, shouty alternative of ALL CAPS.

Use Title Case in your short description headlines.

So What?!?

A good way to test your copy to see if it is going to be engaging and motivating is to carry out the 'So What?' test.

Ask 'So What?' after each statement. Relate it back to the *Moving Away From Pain* or *Moving Towards Pleasure* goal you identified.

"It's got 3 bedrooms."

"*So What?*"

"You can have a study and a guest room."

"*So What?*"

"When friends come to stay you don't have to shift all your work stuff from the spare room into the living room."

"*So What?*"

"It'll save you time. You can get on with your work without worrying about getting distracted. Or worry about getting in the way when everyone else is catching up."

"So What?" comes into it's own if you've given detailed thought to the ideal Buyer or Tenant for your property. If you've identified the #1 reason why they're looking to move.

You might think this is all unimportant 'Woo Woo' stuff. All that flowery nonsense won't make much difference to how many people click or request a viewing.

Statistics prove that you couldn't be more wrong.

Chapter Summary

- Your Short Description Summary is your Headline
- Move your reader towards pleasure or away from pain
- Ask them questions or get them thinking
- Get your reader saying 'That's Me!'
- Briefly backup your main claim
- Don't waste a single character
- Use the 'So What?' test
- Use Title Case

CHAPTER 9 – THE FULL DESCRIPTION

"A good headline gets your foot in the door of the reader's mind. An unfortunate lead paragraph can cause you to lose a couple of toes."

Howard Newton, JM Mathes Inc.

Your first paragraph should continue the ideas expressed in the Short Description headline. That's what attracted them and got them clicking in the first place.

Similar to when you're doing a Google or Facebook Ad, the landing page needs to mirror what the person has already seen in the Ad…

Give them more than they got in the Short Description, to reward them for clicking through.

The first paragraph needs to be short, punchy and easy to read. The Short Description headline 'sold' the click. The first paragraph needs to convince the reader to continue reading on.

With a face to face sales appointment you can respond 'live' on the fly. You can answer your prospects questions and focus on their most pressing needs, their urgent pain points.

You can't react and respond with an ad, direct mail piece or a property listing. You have to consider every objection, every query, every pain point in advance.

Having done this you put your response down in words, so it's there if needed.

Don't get me wrong – doing all that isn't easy.

Most agents give up before they've even started. Instead they plonk down a list of facts and bullet points into the full description. Then they complain that no one ever reads it so it doesn't make a difference anyway...

So these tried and tested copywriting principles work in 99.9% of all other industries around the world, helping to sell everything from chewing gum to super yachts...but the UK property market is different...?

Consider this for a second.

Imagine you were on trial for murder.

As part of this trial how many character witnesses would you like called? How long would you give them each to talk about you?

How about limiting it to one friend with only 10 seconds to read a list of bullet points!?

Most people would want to bring in everyone they could think of.

Most people would want them to wax lyrical about their virtues, tireless charity work and good character!

So why should a property listing be any different? Why cap your potential to persuade?

Language & Style

It's worth pointing out a few copywriting basics that can make a big difference to your writing.

First, forget everything you learned at school about what 'good' writing looks like.

At school, I would proffer that you were handsomely honoured and recognised for the use of verbose polysyllabic pronouncements of complex formulation.

You What!?

You were told to write in a formal and pompous style. A style completely at odds with how people actually communicate with each other.

Estate Agents tend to be quite good at this stuffy style of writing. And that's nothing to be proud of!

Write as you speak. Use simple words, the simpler the better. Use short sentences. Write short paragraphs – try to keep them to a couple of sentences at most.

Big blocks of text can look scary and off-putting. See how I rarely have a paragraph more than 3 sentences in length?

And don't be afraid to start a sentence with 'And'.

Next, ditch the jargon.

Your reader is not a property industry expert. You should ensure that your reader understands every word you write. Jargon puts a MASSIVE barrier in the way of that understanding.

People don't like to feel foolish or like they the only ones who aren't in the know.

One acronym or buzz word could be all it takes for them to click away, never to return again.

Have you ever stopped to think what "Well Presented" actually means!?

Readability

There are free online resources to make your copy more readable and understandable.

I like **www.hemmingwayapp.com** which ranks your copy by US school grade reading age. It also gives visual pointers for how to improve readability and clarity.

I've used it throughout this book. That includes the example listings in chapter 13. I've aimed for US school grade 4 – 6, which is 9 – 11 year old.

I'm not saying any of my readers have the reading age of a nine year old…just it's been proven to be the most accessible in terms of readability, speed, ease & understanding.

Major Advantages, Not Minor Claims

It's tempting to dump everything you know about the property into the listing. This may not be the most effective approach.

There might be a place for everything you know about the property. You just need to know where to put it.

Remember that the role of the listing is to get the viewing request.

People buy on emotion and justify with logic.

Based on my own unscientific research I'd say that 90% of all property ads are 90% factual.

Very few even touch on the emotional side. Yet we know that the most persuasive arguments are emotional, backed up with a few choice facts.

You'll all know from experience that buyers will often get a feeling about a property.

They step inside and immediately know it's 'The One'. Often that's regardless of the square footage, location or the worktop material.

Focus on what's going to emotionally influence your target Buyers or Tenants.

Think about the most important pain points your ideal Buyer or Tenant is looking to remove. Or the pleasure they are seeking to gain. Focus on THAT.

This isn't any different to the thought process behind the Short Description headline. But here you aren't limited to 250 characters.

What do people really want when you get under the surface? Here's a list as a reminder:

- Better Health
- More Comfort
- More Money
- More Leisure
- Greater Popularity
- Pride or Accomplishment
- Improved Appearance
- Business Advancement
- Social Advancement
- Security in Old Age

- Praise From Others
- Increased Enjoyment

Chapter Summary

- Focus on the Major Advantages and the impact they will have on their daily lives
- Write simply and clearly. As you'd speak to a friend
- Always check your readability score

CHAPTER 10 – COPY LENGTH

There's always a lively debate when it comes to discussions over copy length. And this isn't limited to property listings.

The long copy vs. short copy discussion goes back 100's of years. It still creates very strong opinions, with few people sitting on the fence.

In summary – some people think that long copy is boring and uninteresting and no one will ever read it. They think it's better to be short and concise.

Others think that you shouldn't limit your creativity. They believe the well written long copy will be more motivating.

In the interests of full disclosure I'm in the Long Copy camp.

The detailed research carried out by US mega-portal Zillow on 24,000 transactions supports this view.

They found longer listings consistently sell for more. They looked at bottom tier, middle tier and higher tier homes.

Across all three categories, the longer listings were much more likely to achieve higher than the expected price.

They found that 250 words was the ideal length to maximise the sale price.

The research showed additional words won't increase the price but they won't hurt the price either.

I've worked with and learned from some brilliant copywriters. Most agree that even when writing a long ad, it's a great exercise to start by writing a short one.

There's a famous quote by the French philosopher and mathematician Blaise Pascal:

"I would have written you a shorter letter, but I did not have the time…"

Making your copy work in short form ensures that you focus on what's important.

You condense your message into the most compelling story where every word counts.

With that in mind, if needs be we can achieve this with a property listing in only four sentences;

- State major advantage
- Provide proof
- Give a reason to grasp the advantage
- Call to action

Using this method you could produce a four line ad for the local newspaper or Gumtree/Craigslist.

If you're planning on writing more than four sentences, the copy length is determined by how far down the path you want to take your reader.

How Far Do You Want The Reader To Get?

- Got My Attention
- Won My Interest
- Carried Me Into 1st Paragraph
- 1st Para Got Me To Read The Full Copy
- Copy Held My Interest, Convinced Me, So...
- It's What I'm Looking For, and...
- I'll Get Round To It...Sometime...
- I Am Going To Arrange The Viewing NOW!

To get the reader to arrange a viewing and maximise price, the sweet spot for a property listing full description will be around 250 -400 words.

Chapter Summary

- There's no such thing as copy that's "Too Long"
- But there is copy that's just "Too Boring"
- Work out the key points to persuade in short form to make your long form copy more powerful
- Aim for 250 – 400 words

CHAPTER 11 – PROVE IT!

So far I've encouraged you to write engaging and motivating copy that taps into the emotions. Copy that addresses the real needs of your target Buyers or Tenants. To move them towards pleasure or away from pain.

There is now a role for copy that backs up the claims you have made.

This should come easy to you. After all, most agents love measurements and facts.

But what you're looking to do here is to give the head reasons to go along with the heart. You need both to persuade someone to act.

Think about how the reader would justify their emotion-based decision to their partner, a friend or family member.

It begins with credibility.

One way to establish credibility is to 'Start Where The Reader Already Is'. State familiar facts that generate trust and confidence in what you're saying.

You hardly ever see lines like the one below in a property description.

That's a pity because it achieves many of the above objectives. It will get your reader nodding in agreement.

"3 bedroom 1950's ex-council properties like this one are well built. They often have bigger rooms and more garden space than modern 3 bedroom properties."

For many, build quality, room size and outside space will be important factors.

I'm not suggesting you lead with the above. But used as 'supporting evidence' in the description, it could be much more motivating than launching headlong into a list of room sizes.

Specifics

The more specific you are, the more believable and motivating the statement will be.

You can be specific through stating exact amounts. How much? How big? How long? How many?

But when doing so always think about what specifics will appeal to your target market.

What's better for a young couple?

"1/2 mile to the local shopping centre"

or

"A 3 minute weekend stroll to your favourite pavement cafe"

That said you need to exercise caution with specifics – all too often I see full descriptions which are full of this level of detail:

Living Room / Dining Room 11' 4" (Max) x 11' 6" (Plus Bay) L Shape 8' 7" x 11' 1" (3.45m (Max) x 3.51m (Plus Bay) L Shape 2.62m x 3.38m)

Double glazed bay to front windows. Double radiator. Laminate flooring. Dining area with double radiator, double glazed French style patio doors to rear garden.

Bedroom 1 9' 11" x 11' 6" (3.02m x 3.51m)

Double bedroom. Double glazed window to front. Radiator.

Whoah! That's too much to take in! You'd be better off having a floor plan rather than listing all those dimensions.

And you can say once and for all whether the property has double glazing or gas central heating. Does a reader really need to know that every room has a radiator?

Stories

One of the most powerful ways to 'Prove It' is through a testimonial or story.

This should be from a previous Owner or Tenant in their own words. Make sure it paints an ideal picture to your ideal future occupier. You don't want the current party animal Tenant recounting wild tales of all night parties when trying to attract a family...

Think about the key things that your ideal Tenant will be looking for. Relate the testimonial to the Short Description summary headline. Is it the local shops and cafes? Outside space for the kids? School catchment areas? Gaining their independence?

If you're struggling to come up with content for the testimonial you could introduce a Q&A style section. What was your favourite thing about living here? What will you miss most? What are your 3 favourite local places to eat?

With 'Prove It' copy you don't need a lot to be motivating and powerful. Too much can actually be off-putting. Use it wisely.

Find Fault

One of the best ways to build trust and increase credibility is by being brutally honest.

When you admit that you can't swing a cat in the galley kitchen it adds weight to your gushing prose about the roomy lounge.

It's a *Pattern Interrupt* – people won't be expecting it.

Your competitors won't take this approach. If you write honest property descriptions you stand a great chance of becoming the local 'trustworthy agent'.

Chapter Summary

- Use relevant facts to back up your claims
- Think about what's important to them
- Stories and testimonials sell
- Find fault to build trust

CHAPTER 12 – CALL TO ACTION

You've written your ad. You've got your reader engaged and interested. You've backed up your claims. Now you need to bring it to a close. You need to tell the reader what you want them to do.

Many salespeople 'leave money on the table' by failing to ask for the sale. Most property listings don't convert to their full potential because they don't spell out the Next Steps.

But before you get to the 'Close' it's worth a quick recap.

One of the most powerful words in the English language is 'because'. Studies have shown that giving a reason for your request dramatically increases the chances a positive response. Even if the reason is pretty weak, it still makes a big difference.

With this in mind it's worth a sentence or two of 'selling summary' at the end to pick up on the key points.

Don't undo all your good work by reverting back to features and benefits. Instead pick up on the key transformation the new Owner / Tenant will enjoy – moving towards pleasure or away from pain.

Then give a reason why they need to respond NOW. Don't leave it up to them to do it 'Sometime'.

Tap into Fear Of Missing Out, genuine scarcity, a date when something will change.

Finally be clear about what you want the reader to do. Usually that will be call to arrange a viewing.

It's OK to give them alternative ways of getting in touch. But you should avoid confusing the issue by asking them to do more than one thing.

If you want them to arrange a viewing, that should be the single Call To Action (CTA). Don't muddy the waters by asking them to do something else, like request more information.

Chapter Summary

- Focus your 'Selling Summary' on the key difference the property will make to their lives
- Be single minded with your Call To Action

CHAPTER 13 – IS IT ALL WORTH IT?

Creating the Ultimate Property Listing will take time and effort. But it will be very worthwhile.

An Ultimate Property Listing will increase your click through rates and viewing requests. You will receive more offers and applications. You will sell or let more properties and do so more quickly.

Secure A Quicker Sale Or Let

Let's run the numbers from the earlier example. Increasing the Click Through Rate from 5% to 7% on a property getting 5,000 views per month.

We've already worked out that will result in five extra viewings each month.

Based on an average 15 viewings to secure a sale, this could mean selling in month one rather than month two.

In a joint agency situation that could be the difference which gets you the deal rather than a competitor. Which brings me neatly on to…

100% Of Nothing

Rightmove research has shown that 60% of properties are sold by the 2nd agent instructed, rather than the first.

I don't know if there's a similar figure for lettings. I do know that you're at most risk of losing a Managed Landlord when their property is empty...

According to the Rightmove figures if you're the first agent instructed there's over a 50% chance that you will earn nothing at all from your efforts.

The difference could be earning 100% of your fee or nothing at all.

If you're instructed on 20 properties a month and sell 40% of them, based on an average fee of 1.5% and a value of £250,000 you'd earn £30,000.

But what if you apply Ultimate Property Listing methods and convert 60% rather than 40%. You'd sell another four properties and earn an extra £15,000– from the same property stock, the same workload.

That's 50% more than you would have earned. And chances are a lot of that can go straight to the bottom line.

We can break this down to each individual Ultimate Property Listing.

If applying Ultimate Property Listing methods increases your chance of securing a sale by 20% as shown above, each Ultimate Property Listing could be worth £750.

Not getting paid is bad enough...but what about your local reputation?

Will the 60% of vendors recommend you to their friends and family if you've not found them a buyer? Chances are they'll be singing the praises of your competitor instead!

Higher Profits - For Less Work

Us Brits love a bit of property. It's a national obsession that ranks just behind moaning about the weather. With that in mind how many portal visitors do you think are serious and how many are just nosey neighbours or Property Porn voyeurs?

It might not please the portals to hear this but serious buyers might actually miss out on their ideal property - because they're deluged by the amount of irrelevant choices to scroll through.

And that's where well written copy that speaks directly to the ideal buyer comes in. Chances are they have specific needs that go beyond the basic portal keyword searches.

This matters because listing copy that addresses the pain they are looking to remove or pleasure they want to gain is more likely to stand out to the IDEAL buyer or tenant.

I'm a lover of the 80:20 Principle and it would be fair to assume 80% of property transactions are driven by fewer than 20% of searchers. It's the Genuinely Interested vs the Tyre Kickers.

But what if you could speak directly to the 20% of the 20%? The Ideal buyers or tenants for YOUR property.

Wouldn't it be better to show the property to two or three Ideal buyers or tenants rather than waste hours dealing with 20 who're only vaguely interested?

Well written copy will particularly appeal to the serious and specific. And all this means there's more chance of achieving the asking price and more chance of earning a profitable fee.

Win With Google

Expanding on the point above, a family searching online – frustrated by the need to scroll through hundreds of portal listings – may Google '3 bedroom family home in Gosforth Academy catchment'.

If your copy contains this 'long tail keyword' (sorry if I'm getting a bit technical) it will appear high up in their search results.

This works with the portals and your own site. Either way, it cuts out their laborious search and is more likely to get serious buyers or tenants with specific needs coming directly to you.

Marginal Gains & Continual Improvements

Despite all this, the Ultimate Property Listing approach isn't a Silver Bullet to solve all your problems. Sorry.

But it *is* a prime example of Marginal Gains Theory – where small incremental improvements combine to make significant improvements overall.

Small changes that make a BIG difference.

If you're receptive to this approach I suspect you will always be looking for ways of improving many different aspects of your business.

And that's exactly how The Ultimate Property Listing should be viewed.

Implementing this approach will take effort and expense (time or money). But the benefit will go beyond mere percentage improvements in your conversions. It will speak volumes about your approach to business in general.

I've heard agents in 'hot' markets comment it's a waste of time to do any more than the bare minimum to Sell or Let a property.

I'd argue that in a 'hot' market where you don't *need* to do this, doing so will have a much more powerful impact on those looking for a quality agent.

Having shiny boots won't directly affect how a soldier engages with the enemy...or put another way...

How you do one thing is how you do Everything.

Pre-Suasion

That's not a typo. The above heading is meant to read *Pre-Suasion* rather than Per-Suasion. It's the title of an excellent book by the renowned professor and 'Godfather of Influence' Dr Robert Cialdini.

And some of Dr Cialdini's writings are particularly relevant to property listings and their role in the wider property market.

I did state at the start of this book that a property listing won't affect what happens during the viewing and won't help you with Sales progression.

Actually that's not strictly true.

Because a listing can affect how the potential Buyer or Tenant thinks about the property long before they set foot inside. And that "pre-framing" can work for you in the background in a very persuasive way.

Cialdini states that it's hard to change what people think but much easier to change *what they think about*.

You have a gap between the initial viewing of the listing and the actual property viewing.

That could be minutes, days or sometimes weeks.

Either way, an emotionally engaging listing will 'warm up' the potential prospect during that gap. It gives you the opportunity to direct their attention or focus to where you want it. Back to solving their problems again.

And that sets the agenda for their subsequent choices.

This is in danger of getting very theoretical and academic so I'll bring it back down to earth.

Your listing can influence the choices made *long after the listing was viewed* by directing what the reader thinks about and perceives as important.

Chapter Summary

- Apply the Ultimate Property Listing method and you WILL sell and let more properties
- You will earn more fees
- Your local reputation will be enhanced
- Your listing can influence what a potential Buyer or Tenant thinks about before the viewing

CHAPTER 14 – THREE ULTIMATE PROPERTY LISTING EXAMPLES

Now it's time to bring it all together.

I've taken three property listings and given them an *Ultimate Property Listing* rewrite.

I've included examples of how you can achieve powerful results for both Sales & Lettings with 250 to 400 words.

The length really depends on the materials you've got to work with. And that's largely determined by the property.

You'd be wrong to assume it needs a bigger executive style home to really get the benefit of the *Ultimate Property Listing* approach. The examples shown demonstrate that you can make big difference across a range of properties likely to appeal to an 'everyday' buyer.

#1 Two Bedroom Flat - Original

Deceptively spacious and modern 2 bedroom first floor apartment in the highly desirable Markby Close, Moorside. Fantastic location nearby many local amenities, popular schools and is within easy access to Doxford International Business Park, the A19 and Sunderland City Centre.

Briefly comprising of entrance hallway to the light and airy lounge, modern kitchen, two good sized bedrooms, master boasting built in robes and contemporary family bathroom. Externally to the front lies a well maintained lawned garden and parking to the rear.

(81 Words)

#1 Two Bedroom Flat - Ultimate Property Listing Method

Could This Be The Ideal Flat To Share With A Doxford International Friend Or Colleague? It's only a 5 minute stroll from the business park - move here and you can steal a precious few extra minutes in bed!

It's got 2 decent sized double bedrooms – so you if you do share, you don't need to fall out over who gets the small room.

Many Moorside flats have old electric storage heaters but this one's has gas central heating! That'll save you money AND give you much more control over your heating.

The kitchen is quite small but it's modern and has everything you need. Chances are you both won't be cooking at the same time anyway. And there's less to clean.

The modern bathroom has a shower over the bath. You can have an invigorating shower in the morning or a relaxing soak after a hard day at work.

It's decorated throughout in an unfussy white colour scheme. With laminate flooring in the lounge and kitchen you don't need to worry about staining the carpets. There is neutral carpet in both bedrooms – so you don't get cold tootsies getting out of bed in on a winter's morning.

Got a car? There's plenty of on street parking to the rear of the property. The flat also comes with it's own front lawned garden. Yes…that means you do have to cut it.

Here's what Barclays worker Alice (26) says about living in Moorside "I love it here because you can walk to work and there's a fantastic David Lloyd gym. You've got Morrisons, Aldi and a couple of decent pubs all within 10 minutes walk."

Moorside flats do get snapped up because they're so versatile. They work well for sharers, singles, couples or even older downsizers.

This is a particularly good example where the landlord has taken great care of it. Priced at only £475pcm (less than £250 a month if you're splitting the rent) we know it's going to be popular.

Call us today on xxxx xxx xxxx to arrange a viewing

(364 words)

#2 Two Bedroom Bungalow – Original

Offered with no onward chain, this impressive two bedroom bungalow is positioned on this ever popular estate of Dinnington Green. The detached property boasts a spacious lounge/sitting room, conservatory and generous gardens. The accommodation briefly comprises: Entrance hallway, lounge/sitting room, dining area, fitted kitchen, conservatory and family bathroom. There are two double bedrooms, each with front aspect views and with built in wardrobes to the Master Bedroom. Externally the property benefits from driveway parking leading to the garage. To the rear is a fabulous mature garden, predominantly laid to lawn. Other highlights of note: Gas central heating, double glazing and Freehold.

(101 words)

#2 Two Bedroom Bungalow – Ultimate Property Listing Method

Make It Your Own Or Flip It – The Choice Is Yours. This bungalow is perfect if you want a 'project' to put your own stamp on a property or are looking to buy, refurb and sell.

It's got 2 double bedrooms but the dining room could become a 3rd bedroom or study. There is scope to have an informal dining area in the main living room, so you could still sit down to a meal.

Chances are you'll want to redecorate and replace the flooring, kitchen and family bathroom. There's scope to reconfigure inside or even extend into the back garden. You could replace the conservatory with a permanent extension to add value.

There's plenty of off street parking – space for at least 2 cars – and a single garage.

The property is on a quiet estate in a growing commuter village. It's handy for Newcastle Airport (3 miles), Gosforth (5 miles) or Newcastle City Centre (8 miles).

For families, there's a brand new First School in the village which feeds Gosforth East Middle School in the Gosforth Academy system.

This property will suit a wide range of occupiers, from downsizers to young families. It offers a great 'blank canvas' to put your own mark on a property. It's priced to sell and there's no chain, so we're expecting a lot of interest.

Call xxxx xxx xxxx to arrange a viewing.

(237 words)

#3 Three Bedroom Semi – Original

Three bedroom Semi Detached house is available on an unfurnished basis. The accommodation comprises: hallway, living/dining room, kitchen and utility room. To the first floor are two double bedrooms and one single and bathroom. Redecorated throughout.

Entrance Hall 6' 2" x 11' 6" (1.88m x 3.51m)

Laminate flooring. Staircase. Radiator. Doors to:

Living Room / Dining Room 11' 4" (Max) x 11' 6" (Plus Bay) L Shape 8' 7" x 11' 1" (3.45m (Max) x 3.51m (Plus Bay) L Shape 2.62m x 3.38m)

Double glazed bay to front windows. Double radiator. Laminate flooring. Dining area with double radiator, double glazed French style patio doors to rear garden.

Kitchen 8' 10" x 10' 6" (2.69m x 3.2m)

Fitted with a range of wall and base units with contrasting worktops. Single stainless steel sink with drainer and mixer tap. Integrated electric oven with ceramic hob. Brush steel filter hood and splash back. Double glazed window to rear aspect. Space for dishwasher and fridge/freezer. Radiator. Laminate flooring. Door to:

Utility Room 7' 2" x 8' 0" (2.18m x 2.44m)

Wall and base units with contrasting work tops. Double glazed window to rear. Double glazed door to rear. Space for washing machine and dryer. Laminate flooring.

Landing 6' 1" x 8' 1" (1.85m x 2.46m)

Double glazed window to side. Storage cupboard. Doors to:

Bedroom 1 9' 11" x 11' 6" (3.02m x 3.51m)

Double bedroom. Double glazed window to front.

Bedroom 2 8' 2" x 10' 10" (2.49m x 3.3m)

Double bedroom. Double glazed window to rear aspect. Double radiator.

Bedroom 3 7' 8" x 8' 5" (2.34m x 2.57m)

Single bedroom. Radiator. Double glazed window.

Bathroom 5' 5" x 8' 7" (1.65m x 2.62m)

White suite. Panelled bath with shower mixer tap and shower screen. Tiling to bath area. Pedestal wash hand basin with chrome mixer tap. Low level W.C. Two double glazed window to rear aspect. Heated chrome ladder style towel rail.

Rear Garden

Laid to lawn with timber fence boundaries. Borders with mature shrubs. Paved patio area. Shed.

Front Garden

Low maintenance with gravel. Block paved driveway. Dwarf wall with wrought iron gates.

Garage

With 'Up and over' garage door.

(376 Words)

#3 Three Bedroom Semi – Ultimate Property Listing Method

A Large 3 Bedroom Semi In Gosforth Academy Catchment For Only £750pcm? How can that be? This is an ideal 'blank canvas' - a neutrally decorated family home on the popular 1970's built Red House Farm estate.

It's only a ten minute walk to Fawdon Metro station. The Metro will whisk you to Regent Centre for Gosforth Academy, GEMS or Gosforth Central in 3 minutes. Stay on for another 10 minutes and you're in the heart of Newcastle city centre.

A large open plan lounge dominates the ground floor. Access to the rear garden is via French doors from the dining room. The fitted kitchen isn't the biggest but you do have a separate utility room for the washing machine and drier.

Upstairs there are two double bedrooms and a decent sized single bedroom. No fitted wardrobes or en-suites, I'm afraid. The modern bathroom has a shower over the bath - giving flexibility that families need.

Out front there's off street parking for 1 car and a single garage to cram full of boxes, gym equipment and bikes. To the rear there's a mature garden with both lawned and paved areas. There's even a shed for the BBQ and mower.

David, Helen and their son Max lived here for 3 years. "We wanted Max to get into the Gosforth schools system but anything near the High Street was too small or too expensive," says David. "We didn't even know that Red House Farm was in the Gosforth Academy catchment area! But this spacious, affordable house has been perfect for us as a family".

Red House Farm is a mostly owner occupied estate, so family homes like this one don't come up to rent too often. That's why they get snapped up fast!

Call us today on xxxx xxx xxxx to arrange a viewing.
(311 words)

CHAPTER 15 – PROPERTY POWER WORDS

I hope by now you're convinced of the many benefits that improving your property listings will bring to your business.

If you're not convinced, think about the extra profits when you sell more properties to the ideal buyer at the asking price.

Compare that to slashing the price to drum up interest (and slashing your fee!)

Think about bucking the trend that sees the first agent instructed sell only 40% of instructions.

Or think about the extra managed properties you'll gain with a local reputation for quality, based on your unique approach to your listings.

The bigger questions are what your time is worth, and does it make sense for you or your team to try and figure this all out for yourselves?

Or do you decide to work with an experienced direct marketing and property professional who'll make sure your listing copy attracts and engages with more ideal buyers and tenants?

Property Power Words is the name of my done-for-you listing copywriting service.

It's where me and my team help agents who want the benefit of well crafted, engaging listing copy - but don't have the time or don't want the hassle of creating it themselves.

I offer a range of affordable and flexible packages, all with a guaranteed 24 hour turnaround.

Just like Domino's, if your fresh, tasty and hot copy isn't with you within 24 hours you get it free! You'll have your unique, powerfully written listing copy online in no time.

It's quick and easy to get me everything we need to create your IDEAL copy. It's all stuff you'll have to hand already, so it's not going to add to your workload.

If you're interested in finding out more, the next chapter 'The Next Step' spells out what you need to do. And it all starts with a quick call to help you decide if working together is a good fit for both of us.

Thank you and I look forward to helping you.

CHAPTER 16 – THE NEXT STEP

Well Done! You've almost finished this book. I hope you can see how to *Create Powerful Estate & Letting Agency Listings To Grow Your Profits*.

More than that, I hope that I've inspired you to think creatively about your business and challenge the normal ways of working.

I wrote The Ultimate Property Listing as a starting point in our relationship. As I see it, you have three options right now:

1. You can close this book and do nothing with the advice I've shared. For you to have read this far I hope that's not an option but let's face it…most people starting this book won't finish it, let alone act on it.

2. You can start improving your listings on your own using the techniques I've shared.

3. There's a simple and easy way to get your property listing copy written in a way that gets immediate results. It all starts with a 15 minute call between you and me. It gives us the chance to 'meet' and to talk about my Property Power Words done-for-you copywriting package, to see if working together makes sense.

There's no obligation, the call is free and what have you got to lose? You've already invested an hour of your valuable time to get to this page in the book, why not invest a further 15 minutes!

Visit the website below to schedule your call:

www.ultimatepropertylisting.com/powerwords

The choice is now yours. Whichever option you take, that's fine with me and I wish you all the best. Whether you take up this offer of a free call or not isn't going to make a big difference to my business...but it could make a huge difference to yours.

Thank you so much for taking the time to read my book. I hope that I've inspired you to take action, improve your listings and grow your business.

If I can be of more help to you (with your listings or growing your business in general) please get in touch.

Neil

Neil Whitfield
neil@neilwhitfield.com

ABOUT NEIL WHITFIELD

Hi, I'm Neil

I'm a business growth consultant, trainer and now, author. I specialise in helping Letting Agents & Estate Agents grow their businesses.

My first 'proper job' after graduating from Sheffield University was in the marketing department of a large regional brewery. Result!

In 1999 I relocated to Manchester. I spent the next 8 years working for multinational marketing agencies on an impressive roster of big brands. During that time I developed successful (and occasionally award winning) direct marketing campaigns.

Previous marketing clients include: McCain, Rolls Royce, RBS, Warburtons, Crown Paints, Aunt Bessie's, Nissan, Energizer, Revolution, Wilkinson Sword, Vileda and Marston's.

In 2007 I left the world of marketing to open a cold-start Letting Agency, back in my native Northeast. It wasn't quite as crazy and random as it sounds..!

Two weeks later the Credit Crunch hit. I used all my marketing and client service skills to get through this nightmare scenario then built the agency into one of the most highly rated and successful in the area.

Having enjoyed 10 years of double digit growth, I sold the letting agency in 2017 to seek a new challenge, namely helping other business owners to succeed.

Now I work with Agents throughout the UK and 'keep my hand in' as a Landlord & Property Investor.

To find out more about me you can visit **www.neilwhitfield.com**

DON'T FORGET YOUR BONUSES!

I hope you've enjoyed reading '*The Ultimate Property Listing*'.

Don't forget that as a Thank You gift I'd like to give you a **FREE Ultimate Property Listing Checklist.**

Each item on the checklist is a helpful reminder of the methods I'll be outlining in this book. I use the checklist myself when creating listings for clients.

And that's not all! You'll also receive a **FREE Bonus Chapter** 'Taking Your Ultimate Property Listing Offline'.

This bonus chapter details how you can quickly and easily repurpose your Ultimate Property Listing to create real standout offline through direct mail.

DOWNLOAD YOUR FREE CHECKLIST & BONUS CHAPTER NOW!

www.ultimatepropertylisting.com/checklist

A SMALL FAVOUR

Thanks for reading *The Ultimate Property Listing*! I'm positive that if you follow what I've written you'll quickly see your listings convert into more viewings, more Sales and more Lets.

I have a small, quick and easy favour to ask.

Would you mind taking a minute or two to leave an honest review of this book on Amazon?

Reviews are the BEST way to encourage others to buy this book and I also check all my reviews looking for helpful feedback.

Visit:

www.ultimatepropertylisting.com/review

Thanks!

Neil

P.S. If you want to order multiple copies of the book or to discuss speaking opportunities please email me at **neil@neilwhitfield.com**

Printed in Great Britain
by Amazon